Online Privacy:
How To Remain Anonymous
and Protect Yourself While
Enjoying A Private Digital Life
On The Internet

Table of Contents

Introduction

I want to thank you and congratulate you for downloading the book, *"How to Remain Anonymous and Protect Yourself While Enjoying A Private Digital Life On The Internet."*

It is no secret that scouring through the digital world not only brings convenience to the world as a whole, but there are many things that you are able to do online today that you weren't able to do a couple of years ago. Not only can you now shop online for virtually anything that you need, but you can enter the world of dating, meet new friends and even find work online. With the digital world we now can stay connected to the entire world as a whole without having to leave the comfort of our own homes. All that you need is a computer and you are set to go.

However, as convenient as this world may be, it still poses its own unique set of dangers. Living behind the walls of a computer will not leave you anonymous and there is enormous risk involved when it comes to keeping all of your personal information hidden from those who would harm it. It is incredibly easy to track down a person today using a computer, that all you literally need is a name and an address.

Although many people today would condemn the act of remaining anonymous online as the only people who do that are those who usually participate in illegal matter, there is a way that you can remain anonymous and safe while scouring the Internet.

In this book you will find a list of solutions and tips that will help you to remain anonymous online and all of them are relatively simple to follow. If you are looking for a way to protect yourself online, this is certainly the book for you.

Thanks again for downloading this book, I hope you enjoy it!

Chapter One: What Is Anonymity and Is It Possible To Achieve It On The Internet?

So, what is anonymity by definition? The act of anonymity is the ability to keep all of your actions, activities or true identity safe and from being known publicly.

There are numerous reasons why the many different entities that we encounter on the Internet today want to find out your true identity in order to find out why you purchases certain objects online, track past purchases and as well as other browsing activities. While these entities are most of the time completely harmless, it is not uncommon for law enforcement officials to track down someone's real identity especially if that person has been previously linked to a crime.

Most of us already have a specific identity to which we go by already and we are known as by our friends, family, banks and government by a specific name and alias. These people can easily identify us by our social security number, the photo on our driver's license, healthy history or reputation.

We all have some kind of public identity to which we go by and the truth is most of us avoid keeping ourselves anonymous simply out of necessity. Why do we do this? It is because it is just convenient. Anonymity is far from convenient and there are times where all we want is convenience. Who doesn't want to do a simple Google search or check their e-mail account without having to go through the trouble of hiding who they really are?

Don't feel bad for wanting convenience, however, don't assume that you will never be able to do anything anonymously. Using the right web browsers or accounts will allow you to conveniently do all of the things that you love to do while on the Internet, while still keeping your anonymity intact.

While the connections and clues that you leave behind whenever you are online are not always followed by people who would use your information harmfully, these breadcrumbs can still be easily found by a variety of government agencies or hackers, especially if they make the effort in order to find out who you really are.

When it comes to anonymity, you need to start straight from scratch, especially if you want to keep yourself safe. The best way to keep anonymity is to make sure that you keep all of your accounts that are connected to your real identity separate from the accounts that are connected to your anonymous identity.

The Different Levels of Anonymity

There are different levels of anonymity that you can achieve and anyone can achieve the specific level that they want as long as they are very creative and have access to all of the right resources. The more you do to safeguard your privacy, the higher level of anonymity that you will have.

To best raise your level of anonymity, you first must ask yourself what specific level do you require? Of course to answer this question you will need to look into the future to anticipate exactly how anonymous you want to remain. If you have some idea of who or what you are trying to protect your identity from and what resources they may have at their disposal, you will be able to enact the proper level of anonymity without going overboard and wasting your own time and resources.

Unfortunately, there is no way to tell exactly whom you are trying to protect your identity from. Sometimes there are overlapping levels of anonymity. They aren't always so cut and dried. That forum troll you offended might happen to be an upper level NSA analyst with access to copious resources. The truth is that you never know.

Chapter Two: How To Thoroughly Clean All Of Your Information Online

Before you can even start thinking about protecting your identity as a whole, you need to fully know what information you have that is already readily available online. You may be surprised to find out how much information there is about you online already.

You may find sensitive information about you lingering on the Internet today such as phone number, email address, full legal name, birthdate and social security number. These are just a small list of things that should not be online for the entire world to see and it is extremely important that you find what is lingering on the Internet so you can get them down before anybody else can see them.

To start looking for your sensitive pieces of information online, follow these easy steps:

1. Check Out What Others Can Find Out About You

To do this conduct a simple search in Google, Bing or Yahoo search. However, in order to do this successfully make sure that you are not logged in to any of your email accounts with these webs browsers or social media sites.. If you are signed into anything the search engine will pick up certain activity based on the information that is stored on your computer.

When you do the search make sure that you look at both the web and images category to see exactly what you can see.

2. Make A List of Everything That You Find

If you find a lot or a little information about yourself online, make sure that you take notes on everything that you find. Write down everything! When making your list make sure that you write down website information, where the information originated from and other related information to the website such as phone number or address if they are available.

3. Remove Any Sensitive Information That You See

If by chance you have a long list of websites that contain your name or other personal information on it, the best thing that you can do is to start off with the most basic websites. Why do you want to do this? Because these small websites could have gotten your information off of other bigger websites such as Google or Facebook.

4. Make Your Facebook Account Private

Most people do not realize that every time they update their timeline or profile in Facebook, search engines are immediately alerted and rank the new information that it receives. However, there is a way to make sure that this does not continue happening for you and all that you have to do is tweak the privacy settings within you profile.

To do this Unlink your timeline from search engines by turning off the "Who can look me up?" feature. Take note that after you turned this feature off, it may take some time, usually 24 to 48 hours, for the search engine to implement it, so you still might see your Facebook profile on the search results.

5. Learn More About Your Google Plus Account

With Google + accounts, there is no way to make your profile private as of now – and it seems like Google doesn't have any plans to add that feature in the future – so the best you can do is put a restriction on it, limiting the public to seeing only your name and profile picture. The option to delete your whole Google + profile is also available, but don't worry, deleting your public profile does not affect your Gmail account, if you have one. Adding restrictions or disabling accounts can be done under the Settings Page.

6. Keep All Of Your Data Protected

The moment that you remove all of your personal and sensitive information off line, it is then your responsibility to ensure that your data stays off the Internet at all costs. There are numerous ways that you can do this and in the next couple of chapters you will learn how this can be achieved.

Chapter Three: Understanding the Importance of Your IP Address and How It Could Inhibit Your Privacy Online

If you have never head of an IP address it simply stands for The Internet Protocol Address. This address is simply a unique set of numbers that identifies your specific computer on the entire network that is called the Internet. To put it in simple terms, your IP address is your address that is used in the virtual world. Without it, you cannot do a thing.

While your IP address does not have information that can tell somebody that you are the person that owns the IP address or that can give away all of your personal information, there are certain ways that agencies are able to get information on you. Under certain laws throughout the US an agency can request to have your personal information directly from your Internet Service Provider. If there are legal papers presented, your service provider won't have any choice but to hand over your information.

Most people don't have a problem with certain legit agencies from requesting their information, but I was certainly not one of those people. Agencies are not the only people out there who want my information or yours. There are other people such as stalkers, scammers and hackers that want the information as well and they are just sitting there lurking in the background, waiting for their chance to grab that information.

How Cookies Play A Role In Your Online Security

What is A Cookie? How does it play a role in how safe you are online? Cookies are essential bits of information that are stored in your computer automatically from the numerous websites that you have visited or that you are logged into. These tiny bits of information could contain personal information about you such as your login information, what your user preferences are and what kind of transactions you have made online in the past.

A cookie helps to make a website remember who you are every time you return to them, which helps to make it easier for you to log onto a site every time you come back. This is also the primary reason why you may see relevant results on your searches.

There are two primary types of cookies that you will come across online: third party cookies and first party cookies.

1. First-Party Cookies-these cookies are ones that come directly from the many websites that you have visited.

2. Third-Party Cookies-these types of cookies usually come from any kind of affiliated sites that you have visited in the past. Typically these are advertisers or promoters that work online that have an agreement with your favorite websites such as YouTube, Facebook or Instagram.

Whenever you sign up for a new website, most of the time within the fine print you will find that your favorite website is allowed to hand over your personal information to the other websites they are partnered with. Most of the time however, the only ones who tend to have your information and will be the most bothersome to you are hackers and scammers.

How to Use Your Computer Anonymously

Now that you fully understand how your personal information can be obtained simply by doing simple tasks online such as visiting your favorite website or shopping, it is time to learn the best direction to use in order to move forward with your online anonymity.

1. Browse the Internet Using the Private Setting or The Incognito Setting

One of the most common pieces of advice you'll get when you want to browse anonymously is to use private browsing or the incognito mode of your preferred web browsers. When you're "private" browsing, the browser does not record any of the sites you visit, so it does not appear on your search history.

However, it does not prevent these visited sites from recording your log and capturing the information you entered, if there is any. Basically, private browsing only protects you from the next person who's going to use the computer, as they might look up your search history.

2. Using Web-Based Proxies

Every time you open a web browser, type a website address, and press enter, you are sending a request to the web server to let you access the site. For the web server to send back the page you requested, it needs your IP address. With this kind of system, it is impossible to keep IP addresses to ourselves; however, there is a method that will hide it. Using web proxy servers does this. A web proxy server is an intermediary between a user's computer and the web. When accessing the Internet, a user's computer will first connect to the web proxy server, and the web proxy server will then send the request to the website the user wishes to be connected   to, consequently hiding the person's IP address. What the website will see is the proxy server's IP address instead.

There are two different ways that you can use web-based proxy servers:

1. Configuring your browser manually in order to access these proxy servers.
2. Use websites that are web proxies to access restricted websites.

3. Use the Tor Also Known As The Onion Router

The first question that you must ask yourself is what is Tor in the first place? Tor is actually one of the most effective ways that you can browse the Internet anonymously. The Onion Router, or as it is most commonly referred to as Tor, is a software that is absolutely free to use and that helps you to maintain anonymity when browsing online. This software has the ability to resist both network and geographical censorship. Because of its capability the government has deemed it dangerous as it can build a pathway in some illegal activities such as terrorism, drug dealing, pornography and arms dealing.

While it has gained such reputation, the creators emphasize that the software is made for whistleblowers, activists, journalists, militaries, law enforcement officers, and other people who have related careers, which might endanger one's life, especially if one is living in a country with an oppressive government.

From half a million, Tor had a massive increase in its number of users after it was revealed to the public by the US and UK spies about the possible problems this program could create. Their daily users increased to four million in just a year.

To run Tor all you need is a Mac, Linux computer, or Windows computer, if you are looking to maintain anonymity. The Tor software works by with encryption, users are only able to hide the content of the message, but not the headers. Headers are the information where a message originated and where it was sent. It can also include the information of the file size sent or requested and the exact time of these activities. Based on this information, an online surveillance system using sophisticated traffic analysis may have a high probability of predicting the content of your message. Message, in this sense, refers to your online activity.

To put it in simple terms, think of how you would lose someone that is following you. Wouldn't you want to take different routes in order to lose this person? Well, Tor works the same way.

4. Using Anonymous E-mail Accounts

When it comes to using anonymous email addresses, even if you give up fake information, which still does not keep your IP address hidden. What does this mean? It simply means that you can be tracked and your personal information can still be found. If the government were concerned about your Internet activities and requested your information, they could get it easily.

To prevent this from happening, the best thing that you can do is create a fake-email address using the Tor browser. When even checking these emails you should always use Tor especially if you do not want your IP address revealed.

How To Create A Fake Email Address

When creating your fake e-mail account, do not use Google or Yahoo. Google does not allow anonymous people to sign up. Yahoo does not support HTTPS protection. Tor and HTTPS should go hand-in-hand for a person to be truly anonymous.

Here are the specific steps to creating a fake e-mail address using your Tor browser:

1. Open up the Tor browser.
2. Access either the MailTor or Mail2Tor service that is hidden within it. These two will serve as your primary e-mail providers.
3. Create an account on either of these two sites. However, make sure that you do not list any information that could be linked to your true identity. Make up everything.
4. Whenever you send e-mails, make sure that any of the content within the e-mail cannot be linked back to you in any way.

Of course it is important for you to understand that each method that you use has its own advantages as well as its own limitations.

Chapter Four: How to Shop Anonymously Online

Have you ever wanted to purchase hosting anonymously so that you can make sure that your website or blog can't be traced back to you? Have you ever wanted to buy something for a loved one but wanted to make sure that other people could see none of your payment information? Ever wanted to buy additional storage for your drop box without connection to your real identity online? Have you ever wanted to purchase an online subscription to an online service but didn't want any information to link back to you?

If so then this is the chapter that you are going to want to pay attention closely to.

Anonymous financial transactions on the Internet are possible, but due to copious new banking regulations in recent years, it can be a pain. The traveling to purchase and pick up prepaid charge cards in person is a hassle. The extra fees are annoying. Figuring out expiration dates and reading the fine print can be a nuisance, but what is your anonymity worth?

When it comes to your anonymity when it comes to your financial transactions, what that means is that there is no trail or real connection to who you really are. While this is something that is almost impossible to achieve when you receive money, it is quite possible when you simply purchasing something online. I am not able to give you advice on how to monetize the Internet, however I can give you a few solutions on how you can make these purchases anonymously.

1. Using Anonymous Credit Cards

While there are thousands of different credit cards out there that you can use today, only a handful of them are truly anonymous. Many of the prepaid cards that you see at your local retailer will ask you for personal information and even many more of them will require you to personally verify that information to ensure you are the person that you say you are.

There are many legal reasons for this such as Section 326 of the Patriot Act, which requires any financial institution to verify your ID in order for you to open an account with them. Just take a look at the fine print if you are skeptical about this.

Don't worry; I won't drag you through all this information just to tell you what is and isn't possible. There are some exceptions that haven't been brought under the rules of Section 326 yet. I'm talking about the very uninteresting-sounding gift cards. While they may not be cool, they do a great job of getting the job done in many situations without requiring you to forfeit your precious personally identifiable information. Sure, they may have their drawbacks, but if you are looking to remain anonymous when making purchases online, this is certainly the method that you want to use.

Some of the downfalls of using gift cards if that many cannot be recharged, carry balances above $ 500, or is used by certain retailers because they may not offer address verification system checks, but anonymity comes with its limitations.

When you register the card online, you should do so from a proxy and use a fictional address that you have stored in the gift card. If an online retailer requires an address for verification, you can provide the fictional one that you used at registration. As with most non-rechargeable gift cards, you may end up with a small, practically unusable balance on the card as it nears the end of its life. I highly recommend that you consider donating that balance to a rights and advocacy organization or a charity of your choosing. Remember, when you give back, you get back in return.

2. Using Bitcoin to Your Advantage

I'm sure that most people reading this book thought I was headed straight for Bitcoin when we entered the Anonymous Financial Transactions section, but it has enough drawbacks to be relegated to 2nd place on the list.

While I love the concept of Bitcoin, it still falls short when it comes to cashing in and exchanging your Bitcoins for your local currency. Somewhere in that process, you have to connect and transfer to a bank account with your real, verified information. The same thing goes for putting your money into the Bitcoin ecosystem. You can't purchase Bitcoins with cash at your local Wal-Mart yet. When you make Bitcoin purchase, the money comes from somewhere and that is usually a bank account with your personally identifiable information attached.

That being said, there are ways to acquire Bitcoins without purchasing them via electronic bank transfer. You can sell items, accept Bitcoin payments, and build up a balance. You can purchase Bitcoins in a face-to-face transaction with a friend or complete stranger who wants to cash out in an anonymous manner without using a typical currency exchange service. You can "mine" them.

Even if the Bitcoins are acquired in an untraceable manner, there is the fact that the Bitcoin collects information with each transaction that it is used for. Bitcoins are pseudonymous, not anonymous like most people believe. The jury is still out as to the practical realities of the usefulness of the collected information when it comes to tracing that back to a real live human being.

Every Bitcoin has a "block chain" that records the address of every wallet that has held it. Every transaction adds another wallet address to the list. The real question remains: can you effectively keep your Bitcoin wallet address from being connected to the real you. This is theoretically possible, but you have to be very careful.

There are many ways to remain anonymous online, even when it comes to making online purchases. Whether you decide to use gift cards or bitcoins, you can retain anonymity while online. There is no need to worry about having your personal and financial information when using these methods and you can still gain the anonymity that you have always wanted.

Chapter Five: The Use of Social Networks and Your Anonymity

I know that while there are some people who simply can't seem to live without their social media profiles, if you are the type of person who is looking to have secure anonymity online, this is one sacrifice that you will have to make.

It is no secret that as human beings, we often crave interaction and bonds with other human beings and now this interaction is even easier to achieve online. I doubt that there is even one person that does not have a Facebook account, Twitter account, Reddit account, Instagram account or Tumbler Account. If you are set on still using all of your social media accounts, then there are a few things that you can do to limit your exposure on them.

When it comes to Twitter or Facebook I know that most of us tend to look at our profiles like bank forms, insisting that we fill out every line with the most accurate information as possible. However, if you want to remain anonymous online, you are going to have to lie on the site or at least put some different information on your profile.

Feel free to use a nickname or even an online handle that many people know you by instead of your real, legal name. Feel free to simply ignore data fields asking for your birthday, phone number, or other information that you don't feel like providing.

There are other things that you can do to ensure you anonymity online. Here is a list of things that you can do:

1. Tweak Your Privacy Settings

When you first setup your account, check out your privacy settings. These settings are often hidden away and confusing, but you should make sure that your information is not publicly viewable. Remember that almost always, your profile photo is public. This photo is often sucked into and used by other services if you sign into them using the social network. This means that your profile photo will often end up being publicly available on the Internet. If you are comfortable with that, pick a photo that makes you look good and put your best foot forward. If not, feel free to use an image that is completely unlinked to you like a simple pattern, a nature photo, or a random photo.

2. Prevent Your Friends from Writing on Your "Wall"

You might also want to make sure that your settings don't allow friends to write on your Facebook wall. I'm sure your friends may mean well, but they may come and post Happy Birthday messages on your wall when you may not want to reveal your real date of birth to all your friends. Well-meaning, yet uninformed friends can innocuously and accidentally reveal other information.

Once you have your privacy settings setup how you want, you should visit your social network profile with your browser in incognito mode. This simulates someone from the general public visiting your profile without being logged in and should show you what information, if any, is publicly visible.

3. Cropping or Blurring Out Your Personal Information

If you want to use images or your information online on your social media profiles, but want to make sure that people cannot use that information in a harmful way, you can simply use free and lightweight programs like Irfanview, which will allow you to blur certain portions of the photo or just crop them out. You could even do this to faces if you don't want them to appear in your social media account.

To do this first, click and hold the left (main) mouse button and drag it to draw a rectangle over the area that you want to blur out. When you have drawn the box over the area you want to blur, press, CTRL + E. This will open the image effects browser. From the list on the left, you should select "Pixelize" and use the slider to make sure that that portion of the photo is appropriately distorted.

4. The Consequences of Sharing Your Photos

One of the most common activities on many social networking sites is sharing photos. While I'm sure that your grandparents are clamoring to see those cute photos of you or your little ones, but what if that fantastic, adorable photo you snapped happens to be of your child waving around your credit card after stealing your wallet? You could obviously, just delete the photo, but there are several things you can do to protect your personal information before sharing the photo.

Often times, you may not necessarily be aware that you are even sharing at all when it comes to photos. Not all phone menus or social network site warnings include the details of the privacy implications of the action that you are about to take. You may end up accidentally sharing a personal photo without even knowing it if you don't take the time to learn the software and sharing mechanisms in advance. The best thing that you can do for yourself is simply checking your settings to ensure that you are not sharing your photos unintentionally.

5. Don't "Friend" Every Person in Your Timeline

If you want to maintain some semblance of privacy and security when it comes to social networking, you should devise your own "friending" policy before starting. Many people seem to get into a race or contest to collect as many "friends" as possible. This is irresponsible behavior when it comes to privacy.

To ensure that your privacy is intact, make sure to create your own special policy of which you want to share your personal information with.

The one thing that you need to keep in mind is that there are always going to be people out there that will want your personal information for their own personal gain, and these people will use social media profile to get it. Remember, not only are potential scammers looking to steal all of your information, but prospective partners and employers can use social media profiles to spy on you as well. To fight against potential discrimination, simply limit how much you use social media profile and place strict privacy settings in place so that nobody can get the information that is most important to you.

Resources & Aids To Assist Your Online Privacy

Tor browser

Password Security Tips

IP addresses Explained

Password Storage Journal

Electronic Password Safe

Kaspersky Online Security Software

Norton Online Security Software

Security Camera Surveillance Bundle

Cryptocurrency (Bitcoin) Explained

Conclusion

There will always be certain information that we just simply want to keep to ourselves so as to ensure our own privacy. However, often our privacy is threatened by those who gain unauthorized access to both our business and personal information that we have online.

Maintaining person online anonymity is a challenge and it is one that every person faces. With the advances in technology today, it is hard to go anywhere on the Internet where our information is not being stored, tracked, duplicated or accessed. No matter what your reasons maybe for wanting to go on the Internet anonymously, we all have the right to fight for our privacy, whether it is out in public or in the digital world.

The information that is stored online while may be infinitesimal, but it can still have the potential to harm us in the long run and is often on sold to other companies that wish to have it. It is ridiculous that most of us stand by while we let corporate giants like Google and Yahoo access our information anytime they want just to make some money off our something that belongs to us.

I hope that by using this book you will be able to start keeping your privacy the way you are entitled to and can start on the path towards maintaining your anonymity.

PS: Turn to the next page for your bonus content ☺

Bonus Content!

As a token of our appreciation Grand Reveur Publications would like to give you access to our exclusive bonus content (including free eBooks!).
You're only a click away from receiving:

Exclusive pre-release access to our latest eBooks
Free Shredded Society eBooks during promotional periods
A method ANYONE can use to publish their own book and make passive income

https://ignorelimits.leadpages.net/grandreveur publications/

As this is a limited time offer it would be a shame to miss out, I recommend grabbing these bonuses before reading on.